CONTINENTS

Australia and Oceania

Mary Virginia Fox

Heinemann
LIBRARY

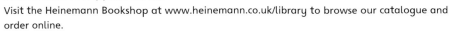

www.heinemann.co.uk/library
Visit our website to find out more information about Heinemann Library books.

To order:

☎ Phone ++44 (0)1865 888066
📄 Send a fax to ++44 (0)1865 314091
💻 Visit the Heinemann Bookshop at www.heinemann.co.uk/library to browse our catalogue and order online.

First published in Great Britain by Heinemann Library, Halley Court, Jordan Hill, Oxford OX2 8EJ, a division of Reed Educational and Professional Publishing Ltd. Heinemann is a registered trademark of Reed Educational and Professional Publishing Ltd.

OXFORD MELBOURNE AUCKLAND JOHANNESBURG
BLANTYRE GABORONE IBADAN PORTSMOUTH NH (USA)
CHICAGO

Designed by Depke Design
Originated by Dot Gradations
Printed by South China Printing in Hong Kong, China

06 05 04 03 02
10 9 8 7 6 5 4 3 2 1
ISBN 0 431 15795 2

British Library Cataloguing in Publication Data
Fox, Mary Virginia
     Australia and Oceania. – (Continents)
     1.Australia – Juvenile literature 2. Oceania – Juvenile literature
     I.Title
     919.4

Acknowledgements
The Publishers would like to thank the following for permission to reproduce copyright material: Earth Scenes/Dani/Jeske, pp. 5, 17; Earth Scenes/Michael Fogden, p. 6; Bruce Coleman/Eric Crichton, p. 8, 21; Peter Arnold/J.P. Perrero, p. 12; Bruce Coleman, Inc./Norman Owen Tomalin, p. 14, 20; Bruce Coleman, Inc./Hans Reinhard, p. 16; Animals Animals/Hans & Judy Beste, p. 15; Peter Arnold/John Cancalosi, p. 19; Photo Researchers/Georg Gerster, p. 22; Bruce Coleman, Inc./Bob Burch, p. 26; Earth Scenes/Paddy Ryan, p.11; Tony Stone/Robin Smith, p. 24; Photo Researchers/Bill Buchman, p. 25; Tony Stone/Doug Armand, p. 27; Photo Researchers/A. Flowers & L. Newman, p. 28.

Cover photo reproduced with permission of Science Photo Library/Worldsat International and J. Knighton.

Our thanks to Jane Bingham for her assistance in the preparation of this book.

Every effort has been made to contact copyright holders of any material reproduced in this book. Any omissions will be rectified in subsequent printings if notice is given to the Publisher.

Contents

Some words are shown in bold, **like this**.
You can find out what they mean by looking in the glossary.

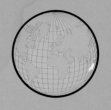

Where are Australia and Oceania?

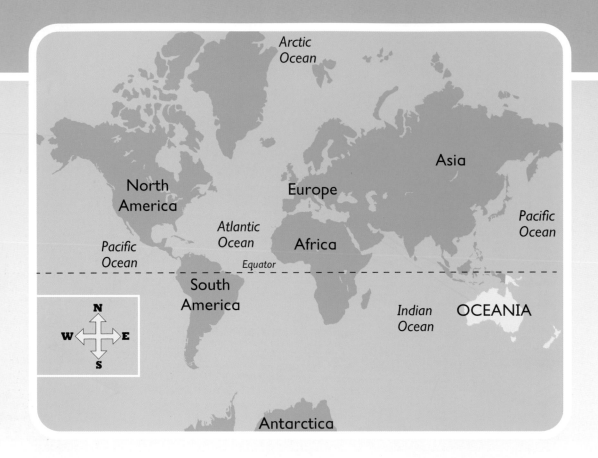

A continent is a vast mass of land that covers part of the Earth's surface. There are seven continents in the world. The huge island of Australia is a continent, but it is also part of a larger group of islands in the Pacific Ocean. This group of islands is known as Oceania. Many people consider Oceania to be a continent.

Australia is by far the largest island in Oceania.

Most of the islands of Oceania lie below the **equator**, in the half of the world known as the **Southern Hemisphere**. However, a group of tiny islands lie north of the equator. This part of Oceania is close to the continent of Asia. Oceania is sometimes also known as Australasia.

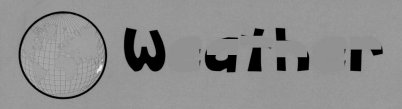

The dry land of the Australian outback

The northern lands of Oceania lie close to the **equator**.
Here, the weather is **tropical** – hot and wet. Steamy swamps
and **rainforests** cover Papua New Guinea and parts of
northern Australia. The weather in most of Australia is very
hot and dry with a short rainy season. The dry, bare
country away from the coast is called the **outback**.

6

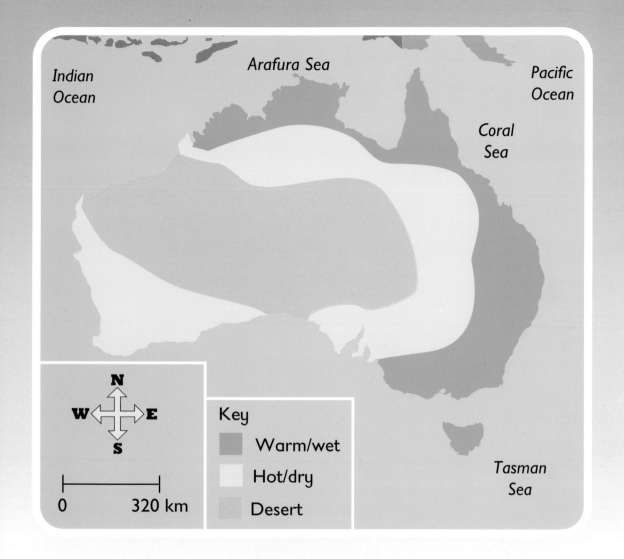

Australia and New Zealand lie in the **Southern Hemisphere**, so their seasons are the opposite of those in the **Northern Hemisphere**. Winter lasts from June to September – the months when it is summer in Europe. New Zealand is closer to **Antarctica** than Australia, and its **climate** is much cooler and wetter.

Mountains

Mount Kosciuszko, Australia's highest mountain

Many islands in Oceania have **volcanoes**, and some of these volcanoes are still **erupting**. Australia has only a few high mountains, but New Zealand has many steep, snow-covered peaks. People go skiing and snowboarding in the Southern Alps, on New Zealand's South Island.

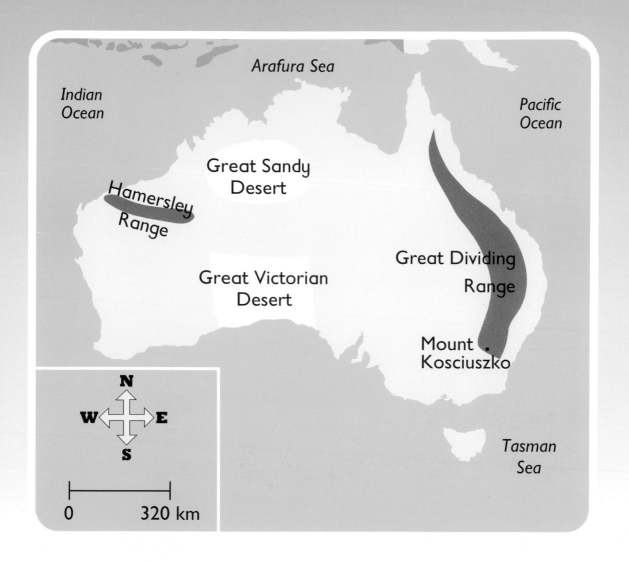

Running along the east coast of Australia is the Great Dividing Range. This long chain of mountains separates the hot, dry land in the centre of the country from the warmer, wetter land along the coast. Most Australians live in cities on the east coast. Very few people live in the harsh deserts of central Australia.

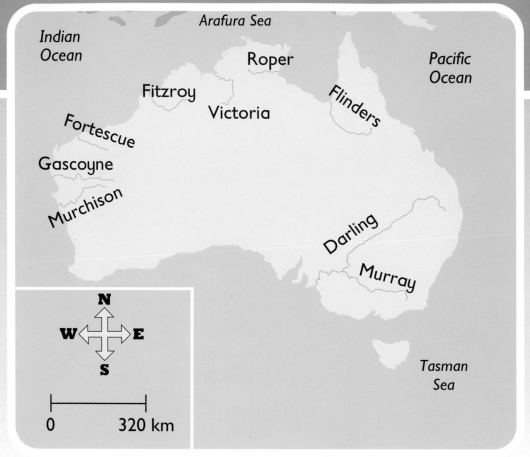

Australia's Murray River flows west from near Mount Kosciuszko to the South Australian coast. On the way, it is joined by the Darling River, which flows from the north. Together, the two rivers make up the Murray–Darling, which is 3750 kilometres long. Some of Australia's best farming land is in the Murray valley.

Murray and Darling Rivers, Australia

Some of Australia's rivers dry up completely during the hot summer months. In contrast to this, many **tropical** islands in Oceania suffer from flooding. Heavy rainfall makes their rivers burst over their banks, often destroying villages and ruining valuable farmland.

Lakes

Lake Eyre, South Australia

Lake Eyre is the largest lake in Australia. It is a **saltwater** lake, and for most of the year it is almost empty. Lake Eyre has only filled up completely three times in the last century. Many Australian lakes dry up for part of the year, leaving dry lake beds covered with salt and clay.

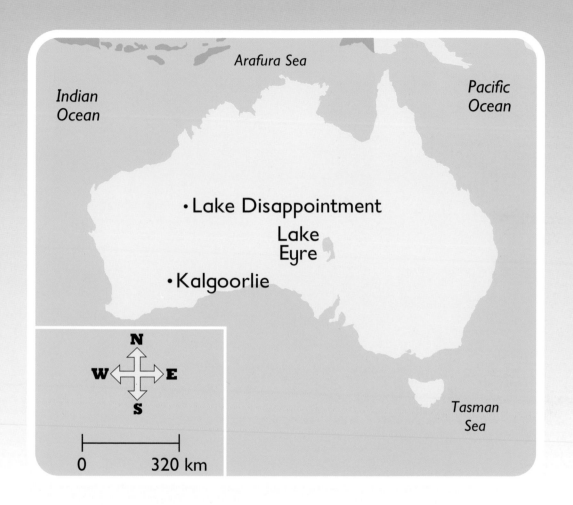

A group of lakes surround the town of Kalgoorlie in Western Australia. In the 1890s, gold was found around these lakes and many people rushed to the area to make their fortune. Further north is the saltwater lake, Lake Disappointment. It was named by early explorers who hoped to find fresh water.

Animals

Galloping emu

Some very unusual animals live in Oceania. The kiwi, in New Zealand, and the emu, in Australia, are both large birds that can run very fast, but cannot fly. In Papua New Guinea, stunning birds of paradise hang upside-down from branches to show off their vivid blue feathers and long tail streamers.

Kangaroo and baby, or joey

Kangaroos and koalas are only found in Australia. They have pouches for carrying their babies. The duck-billed platypus lives near rivers in eastern Australia and Tasmania. It has webbed feet and a flat bill, like a duck. Although it is a **mammal** that feeds its babies with milk, it lays eggs, like a bird or a reptile.

Plants

Eucalyptus trees

Eucalyptus trees grow in many parts of Australia. They are also known as gum trees. There are more than 500 kinds of gum tree. In the **tropical** islands of Oceania, farmers grow sugar cane, bananas and pineapples. In cooler New Zealand, there are farms for kiwi fruit, apples and apricots.

Kangaroo paw

Wild flowers, like the bristly kangaroo paw, grow in western Australia during the rainy **season**. In Australia's scorching deserts, a plant called Sturt's desert pea only blooms after rain has fallen. Its seeds can lie in the ground for many years, waiting for the next rainstorm.

People

Aboriginal children

Around 40,000 years ago people from Southeast Asia began to arrive in northern Australia. They walked most of the way on land that is now under water. Thousands of years later, people began sailing to the Pacific islands. Eventually, some people called the Maoris reached as far south as New Zealand.

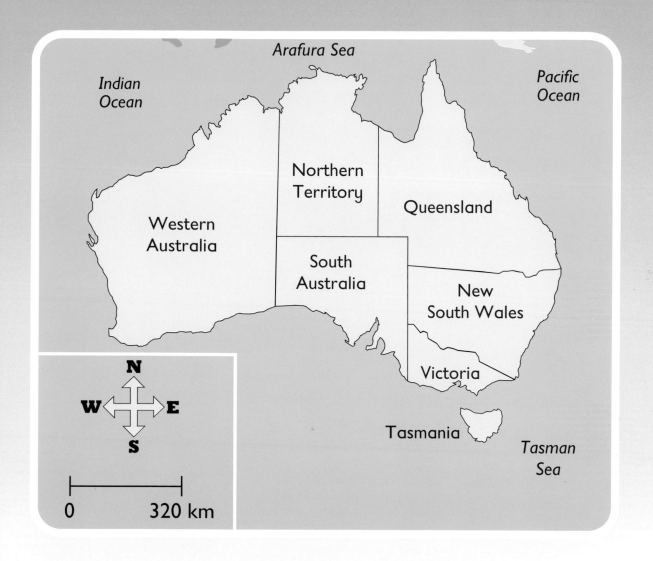

The people who settled in Australia are known as Aboriginals. They lived in Australia for thousands of years before any Europeans arrived. In 1770 the British explorer, Captain James Cook, reached Australia. After this, many people came from Europe to live in Australia. They divided the land into six areas, each with its own **governor**.

Cities

Suburban Australian home

Most Australians live in cities along the coasts. Some people live in flats or houses close to the city centre, but most people have their homes in the **suburbs** surrounding the cities. Because there is plenty of room in Australia, houses are not built close together and they are usually surrounded by gardens.

Melbourne, Victoria

Melbourne is the second largest city in Australia and the capital of Victoria. It was built with money from gold **mining** and is now an important centre for art, the theatre and music. Melbourne has three universities, as well as many offices and factories. Electric trams run through the city centre.

Perth, Western Australia

Perth is the largest city on Australia's west coast and the capital of Western Australia. People sail large **yachts** in the sea around Perth, and many sailing races are held there. New Zealand's largest city is Auckland. It is another popular centre for yachting. It has two harbours and is known as the 'city of sails'.

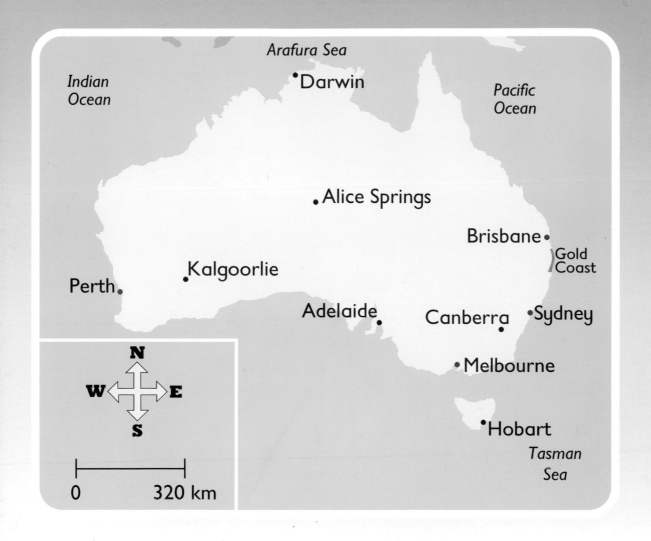

Arafura Sea

Indian
Ocean

•Darwin

Pacific
Ocean

.Alice Springs

Brisbane•
)Gold
Coast

.Kalgoorlie

Perth.

Adelaide.

Canberra
.

•Sydney

• Melbourne

•Hobart

Tasman
Sea

N

W E

S

0   320 km

This map shows some of the most important cities in
Australia. Canberra is Australia's **capital city**. The
government meets there in a modern parliament
building. Darwin is a busy port and a centre for **mining**.
The area to the south of Brisbane is called the Gold
Coast. It has beautiful beaches and many large hotels.

River running through the outback

Away from the cities, the bare land of the Australian **outback** stretches for thousands of kilometres. For centuries, Aboriginals wandered through the outback, using spears and **boomerangs** to hunt for their food. Now, large areas of this land are used for farming. Cattle and sheep farmers live on huge farms, called **stations**.

24

Teaching from a radio station

Most children in the outback live too far away from towns or villages to go to school. Instead they learn their lessons by listening to the radio or using a computer. If people become ill in the outback, they are visited by 'flying doctors' who travel in small planes to see their patients.

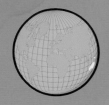

Sydney Opera House

The Sydney Opera House sits on the shores of Sydney Harbour. The sail shapes of its roof were made to look like the sails of **yachts** in the harbour. Sydney is the oldest and largest city in Australia. The Olympic Games were held there in the year 2000.

Uluru, or Ayers Rock, in central Australia

Uluru is a mountain of red rock in central Australia. At sunset, it seems to turn a deep purple colour. Uluru is a **sacred** place for the Aboriginal people and has many rock paintings on its surface. Uluru is its Aborginal name.

Coral and fish in the Great Barrier Reef

Stretching along the northeast coast of Australia is the Great Barrier Reef. It is the world's largest coral **reef**. Coral is made from the skeletons of millions of tiny sea creatures, and grows in many shapes and colours. Thousands of different kinds of fish swim among the coral.

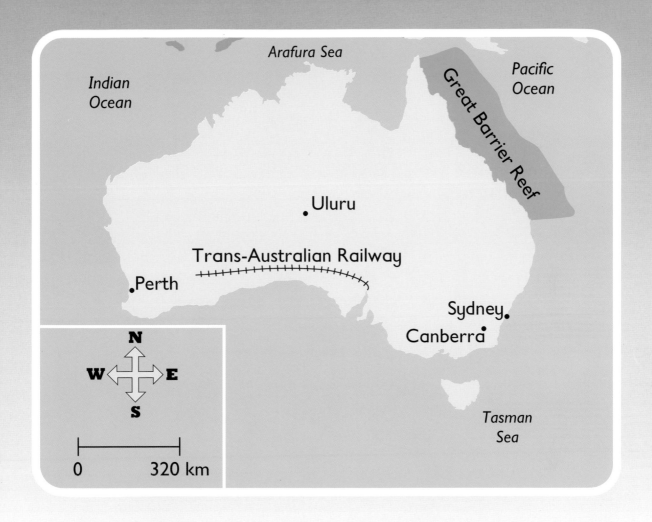

For thousands of years, only the Aboriginal people travelled through central Australia. But in the 19th century European explorers began to cross the **outback**. In 1917 the Trans-Australian Railway was completed. Now a railway runs all the way from Sydney to Perth, but many people travel by plane between cities.

1. There are over 25,000 islands in Oceania, but only a few thousand have people living on them.

2. The islands of Oceania form three groups – Melanesia, Micronesia and Polynesia. Melanesia, which includes Papua New Guinea, lies to the northeast of Australia. Micronesia, which includes Nauru, is north of Melanesia in the west Pacific Ocean. Polynesia, which includes New Zealand, is in the east Pacific Ocean.

3. Many islands in Oceania were made by volcanoes erupting under water millions of years ago.

4. The country of Papua New Guinea, in Oceania, takes up half the island of New Guinea. On the other half of the island is Irian Jaya, which is part of the continent of Asia.

5. The highest mountain in Oceania is Mount Wilhelm in Papua New Guinea. It is 4509 metres high.

6. Australia produces a quarter of the world's wool. There are about ten times as many sheep as people in Australia!

7. Towns in the outback of Australia can be over 150 kilometres apart.

Glossary

Antarctica continent around the South Pole

boomerang curved stick thrown through the air which returns to the thrower when it misses its target

capital city city where government leaders work

climate kind of weather a place has

reef line of underwater rocks or coral close to the surface of the sea

equator imaginary circle around the exact middle of the Earth

erupt throw out rocks and ash

governor someone who runs a country or part of a country

mammal an animal with hair on its body that feeds its babies with milk

mining digging up things from under the Earth's surface

Northern Hemisphere half of the Earth north of the equator

outback land in Australia away from the cities

rainforest thick forest that has heavy rain all the year round

sacred treated with honour and respect

saltwater water with salt in, like the sea

Southern Hemisphere half of the Earth south of the equator

station very large farm where animals are kept

suburb area of houses at the edge of a big city

tropical hot and wet

volcano hole in the earth from which hot, melted rock is thrown out

yacht sailing boat

More books to read

A Visit to Australia, Rachael Bell, Heinemann
   Library, 1999

Step Into Australia, Fred Martin, Heinemann
   Library, 1998

Picture a Country: Australia, H. Pluckrose,
   Franklin Watts, 2001

Index